Ten Short Stories for Lear

EASY READING
for ESL Students

BOOK 5

by Johnny Bread

CANADIAN LANGUAGE SCHOOL

INTRODUCTION

Easy Reading for ESL Students – Book 5 is a comprehensive reader designed especially for intermediate and advanced students of English as a Second Language. The book was developed and tested by full-time teachers of English.

There are ten short stories. Each story is designed to engage students in a well-rounded language learning experience. There are comprehension, vocabulary, speaking and writing exercises after each story.

The stories are entertaining and have plot twists and surprise endings. Teachers of English as a Second Language will enjoy using them to engage students on a wide range of topics and interests.

The stories are short (1500 – 2000 words). Each story and its exercises can be completed in 90 minutes.

You can download a free audio version of the book read by a professional actor. See page 93.

CONTENTS

Jaws	4
The Gypsy	12
The Firefighter	21
Sootie	30
The Enchanted Forest I	40
The Enchanted Forest II	49
The Enchanted Forest III	58
The Texas Rose I	65
The Texas Rose II	74
The Texas Rose III	84

JAWS

It was midnight December 23rd, and little Matthew was not sleeping. He couldn't sleep. He was too excited. Christmas was coming, and there was a fish in the bathtub. His father had bought it and put it there. He did it every year. He always wanted to have fresh fish for Christmas dinner. But this year Matthew was already a big boy. He was five years old and had many good ideas. His newest idea was to play with the fish in the bathtub while his parents and his sister were sleeping. Matthew got up and tiptoed into the bathroom. He closed the door behind him and listened to see if he had woken anybody up. Nothing, everything was quiet. It was dark, but he could see the fish in the bathtub because the moon was shining through the window.

"Hi Fish," he said. You can't sleep either. I can see that."

The fish opened its mouth a few times and looked at Mathew. "Can you talk?" Matthew asked and put his hand in the bathtub. He will never forget what happened next. The fish jumped out of the bathtub splashing water everywhere. Matthew turned around and began to run away, but he slipped on the wet floor. He hit his head on the sink and fell to the floor. Suddenly everybody in the family was awake. His father took him to the hospital. The doctor had to put seven stitches in Matthew's head, but otherwise he seemed to be alright. But he was not.

During Christmas dinner Matthew cried and cried. He couldn't eat the fish. He couldn't even touch it or look at it. From that time fish became a part of Matthew's nightmares. His parents took him to a psychologist. She diagnosed him with ichthyophobia – an irrational fear of fish. "It might go away later in his life," she said. But it didn't go away.

Matthew grew up. He went to see many psychologists, but nobody could help him. "Just avoid damn fish," his friends told him. And so he did. He avoided fish as much as he could. He never looked at them, let alone ate them. If he saw fish, he got scared and ran away. His friends made fun of him, because for them it was comical. But for poor Matthew it was a very serious matter.

The years went by and Matthew didn't get any better.

One extremely hot summer his friends persuaded him to go to the Mediterranean Sea with them for a few days. It was in another country and quite far, so at first he didn't want to go with them. But in the end he said, "I'll go with you, but I won't swim or sail with you."

"Excellent," his friends said. You'll clear your mind a little bit, and who knows what will happen."

So Matthew went with his friends even though he was not very thrilled about it.

On the first day his friends went sailing and fishing. Matthew didn't go with them, of course. They didn't even try to persuade him. He went for a walk around the picturesque little town and enjoyed himself. He took a lot of pictures, had a cup of coffee in a small café and talked to the locals. He was having a good time even though he was alone. It was late in the evening when he decided to return to his hotel. He had started to walk back when he saw a group of men on the street. They were laughing and yelling at somebody. He walked closer, and he knew immediately that something was not right. Four men had surrounded a young woman and were teasing her. The men looked local, and the woman was obviously a tourist like Matthew. He could tell by the way she looked. The woman was not comfortable and needed help, but nobody seemed willing to help her. Matthew decided to act.

"Irene!" he yelled. He looked angry. "Where have you been? I've been looking for you."

The men turned and looked at him. Matthew was a tall man and looked strong, but he was outnumbered. That was obvious.

"You should've called me, Jerry!" the woman shouted. "Don't you have a phone?"

Matthew walked up to the woman, put his arm around her and pulled her away.

The men mumbled something and decided to let them go.

"We don't even know each other," Matthew said when they were far enough away. "And we're already fighting." Isn't this a nice relationship?"

They both laughed. "Thanks a lot," the woman said. "And by the way, you've forgotten my name. I'm Ellen not Irene."

"And I'm Matthew not Jerry, silly." They laughed again.

Matthew walked with Ellen and by the time they got to her hotel, they knew a lot about each other. Matthew liked Ellen a lot, and she seemed to like him too. "What about a drink?" he suggested.

"It's too late," she said." I'm pretty tired."

"OK, never mind. Bye for now." He couldn't hide his disappointment.

"Wait," she said. "Are you free tomorrow night at 6 o'clock? We could have dinner together. I'll pay."

"Let me check my schedule," Matthew said. He took out his phone and pretended to check something. "OK," he said and smiled. I'll meet you here."

The next day they went out to dinner together. They had many things to say to each other. They had a wonderful time. Then it was almost time to leave.

"I was wondering," Ellen said suddenly. "If you are free tomorrow, we could rent a boat and sail to that island over there. I want to go, but I don't want to go alone. What do you say?"

Matthew swallowed hard. His face went white. "I…you know, I…"

"Busy schedule, huh?" she said. Now she couldn't hide her disappointment.

"Yes," Matthew said. "No, I just…"

"Don't say anything," she said. "It's OK. I understand."

Matthew was silent for a minute. *You don't understand anything.* He was thinking hard. His face went from white to red. "I'll go with you," he said suddenly.

The next day Matthew showed up at her hotel wearing special sunglasses. He could hardly see. They rented a boat and started sailing to the island. Ellen was at the helm. Matthew pretended to have a headache and kept his eyes closed most of the time.

"I'm so sorry about your headache," Ellen said.

"I'll be alright when we get to the island," Matthew said.

"Are you seasick?"

"Don't worry about me," Matthew said. He sounded angry, and he felt bad about it. Ellen looked at him, but didn't say anything.

They got to the island and had a nice time together. Matthew felt much better and apologized for being grouchy on the way there. But he had yet to survive the way back. He didn't know what fate had in store for him.

On the way back Ellen suddenly turned off the engine and stopped. "I feel like swimming," she yelled. She took off her clothes and jumped into the water. "Come on Matthew, jump into the water too!"

"I think I'll pass on that," Matthew said. "I don't feel like swimming."

Ellen was evidently enjoying herself. Matthew prayed for this adventure to end as soon as possible.

Then two things happened almost at the same time. Matthew spotted something in the water. He took his sunglasses off. Yes, he was sure of it. It was a fin!

"Shark!" he yelled. "Come back, Ellen, quickly!"

"I can't!" Ellen yelled. "I have a cramp! Help!"

Matthew looked for the life preserver. Where was it? There! He ran to get it. But it was hooked to the boat. He was so nervous that he couldn't unhook it. "Damn it!" he yelled. "Are they stupid to hook it like that!?"

"Help!" Ellen yelled.

Matthew's worst nightmare had just come true. He heard his father. *You're a coward, Matthew. You'll never be a real man.* "No, I'm not!" he yelled. And I'll prove it to you!" He jumped into the water and helped Ellen into the boat.

Ellen was safe. They were both breathing heavily. Then a dolphin jumped out of the water and laughed. Ellen laughed too. "There's your shark," she said happily and laughed again.

Matthew laughed too. "I'm laughing?" he said to himself. I'm not supposed to laugh. I'm supposed to be scared." But he wasn't scared anymore. He was happy to be alive. He was happy to be with Ellen.

When they stopped laughing, Ellen suddenly became serious. "Thanks, Matthew," she said. "You're my hero forever."

He looked at her for a long time, but didn't say anything. He only smiled.

"Tell me something, Matthew," she said after a while. "You weren't scared to die when you jumped into the water? You thought there was a shark, didn't you?"

It took him a moment. Then he said, "No, I wasn't scared."

"Really?" she said incredulously.

Matthew laughed. "Yes, I was. I was so scared. You have no idea."

I. **Complete the sentences with the words from the box below.**

| ~~tiptoed~~ | persuaded | picturesque | teasing |
| grouchy | pretended | mumbled | outnumbered |

1. Matthew walked quietly and carefully on his toes not to wake anybody up. He _tiptoed_ into the bathroom.

2. Matthew didn't want to go to the Mediterranean Sea, but in the end his friends _____ him to go.

3. The town was pretty and interesting. It was located by the sea. It was a _____ little town.

4. The men were laughing at the woman, and she felt embarrassed. They were _____ her.

5. There were four men. Matthew was alone. He was _____.

6. The men said something in a low voice. Matthew couldn't understand. They _____ something.

7. Mathew didn't have a headache, but he acted as if he did. He _____ to have a headache.

8. Matthew apologized for being in a bad mood. He apologized for being _____.

II. **Choose two words from the box on the previous page and write a short paragraph using them.**

_____

_____

_____

_____

III. **Complete the sentences with the expressions from the box below.**

in store	let alone
never mind	pass on

1. Matthew never looked at fish, _____ ate them.

2. Ellen didn't think it was a problem that Matthew couldn't come with her. She said, "_____."

3. Matthew had no idea what fate had _____ for him.

4. Ellen wanted Matthew to swim with her, but he said he would _____ that.

IV. **Choose two expressions from the box above and write a short paragraph using them.**

_____

_____

_____

_____

V. Answer the question in full sentences.

1. Why was Matthew afraid of fish?
2. How did he cope with his problem?
3. Where did he go with his friends?
4. How did he meet Ellen?
5. Where did Ellen want Matthew to go with her?
6. What idea did Ellen get on the way back?
7. What did Matthew see in the water?
8. What did he think it was?
9. How did he overcome his fear?

VI. Oral Summary

Retell the story in a few sentences.

VII. Written Summary

Write a few sentences to summarize the story.

_____
_____
_____
_____
_____
_____
_____
_____

THE GYPSY

Harry Hunter slowly drove his car into a rest stop. He had been driving for two hours, and he was tired and sleepy. He just needed a cup of coffee and a sandwich. He hadn't slept very well last night, and he was hungry. He pulled into a parking spot. I'll be alright in a couple of minutes, he thought. And then I'll be on my way again. He killed the engine, but stayed in the car. He didn't move. He was thinking very hard about something. His face was somber.

Suddenly somebody knocked on his window. It pulled him out of his gloomy dreaming. A young gypsy was standing next to his car. She was saying something, but Harry couldn't hear her. He opened the window.

"Can I help you?" he asked.

The woman laughed. "It's not me who needs help. It's you."

"What are you talking about? Harry asked.

The woman laughed again. "You know what I'm talking about."

Last night Harry had had an argument with his girlfriend. They had been arguing a lot lately. She wanted him to live with her in another part of the country, but Harry hadn't decided yet. He was on his way to talk to her about it, and he felt miserable.

She can't possibly know about my troubles, Harry thought. She's just bluffing. He knew these gypsies at rest stops. They hung around and bothered people with their fortune telling. She just wanted to make some money with her stupid predictions. He didn't need it – not now. He wanted some privacy. He wanted to get rid of her as soon as possible.

Harry opened his mouth. He was going to tell her politely that he didn't need his fortune told. He was in a hurry and didn't have time for it.

"It's going to be all right," she said suddenly. "Don't worry about it anymore."

"What?" Harry asked. He was irritated now. "What the hell are you talking about?"

She smiled at him showing her perfect teeth, and started to walk away.

Harry got out of the car. He watched her leaving. "Wait!" he called to her. She turned around and looked at him.

Something had changed in Harry's mind. He suddenly felt much better. He didn't understand it. Did he believe her? He pulled out his wallet and took a hundred-dollar bill out. He handed her the money.

"Take it," he said. "I don't know how you knew it, but you made me feel much better. I think you might bring me luck. You deserve it."

She took the money, but she blushed slightly. "It's too much," she said.

"Take it," he repeated. "I don't feel bad anymore, so you shouldn't feel bad either."

"What's your name?" she asked.

"Harry, he said. "And yours?"

"Arana," she said. "Good luck to you, Harry. I hope I made your day. You won't regret it." She walked away slowly. Harry watched her.

"I certainly hope so," he said to himself.

Two hours later Harry pulled into his girlfriend's driveway. She was waiting outside for him.

13

"Harry!" she called out and ran to him. She hugged him tightly. "I'm so sorry. I'm so happy you're here. I thought about everything. You were right and I…"

He put his finger to her lips. "Shh," he said. "We're not going to talk outside, Kathy. Let's go in."

They worked everything out. Kathy moved into Harry's house. It looked like a bright future was waiting for them.

Was it the gypsy who made it happen? Harry thought. No, it's not possible – just pure chance.

A year went by, and Harry's life with Kathy was better than ever. He didn't seem to have any problems.

One day Harry's brother George called. He wanted to visit him. He said it would be just a friendly brother to brother chat, but Harry knew better. His brother hadn't visited him for almost a year, and when he came, he always needed something. And Harry was right.

"You're a good businessman, Harry," his brother said after some small talk. "And I'm a good businessman too. Why don't we do business together? We could get a bigger loan and do something really big."

Harry liked his brother very much, but he also knew him very well. He was a little bit wild. So he must be very careful about doing anything with him.

"I'll think about it," he said after a while. "And I'll let you know."

Harry thought about it. He was considering the pros and cons, but he couldn't decide. Then an idea struck him.

The gypsy! he thought. She could help me. But then, he thought, am I going crazy? The gypsy knows nothing about business. How could she help me?"

"She helped you once," his inner voice said. "She could help you again."

Harry didn't say anything to anybody about the gypsy, not even to Kathy. It was his secret.

One Saturday morning he drove to the rest stop and found Arana. She was there telling fortunes.

"Can I talk to you for a few minutes?" he asked her.

She smiled at him. She remembered him. "How did it work out last time, Harry?" she asked.

"Very well," Harry said. "And that's why I'm here. I need your help. But I don't want to talk in the parking lot. Come and have a cup of coffee with me."

"And a piece of cake?" she asked smiling.

Harry told Arana about his dilemma.

"Show me your hand," she said.

Harry showed her his hand. She looked at it for a long time, and then she said, "Now tell me more about your business."

"Well, it's complicated, and I'm not sure you'd understand."

"Well, try me," she said. "Make it as simple as possible."

"I'm a business man," he started. "I make boats and sell them. My brother wants to do business with me. He wants to take out a big loan and make bigger and better boats."

"How is the business doing now?" she asked.

"It's not a great business, but I think I'm doing fairly well."

"Show me your hand again," she said. She looked at it.

"Here's your answer," she said. "Don't do business with anybody – certainly not with your brother. That's all I have to say." She stood up and walked away.

Harry didn't do business with his brother. Later he found out that his brother was deeply in debt. He had lost his business and his house too. Harry had to help him and give him a job in his small company.

So the gypsy was right again! Harry thought. It's unbelievable. Was it all just by chance?

Another year went by. Harry hadn't thought about the gypsy for some time. He was a very happy man. He didn't need her. But today she was on his mind again. Why? Harry was going to propose to Kathy. Wasn't he sure it was the right thing to do? Of course he was. But he was going to ask the gypsy what she thought – just for fun.

"Show me your hand," Arana said. She looked at Harry's hand for a long time. Harry got a little nervous.

"Is something wrong?" he asked.

"Tell me something about her," she said.

Harry started to talk about Kathy. She was watching him. When he finished, Arana took his hand again. She looked at it. "Marry her," she said. "She's the one for you."

Harry was very happy. "But why did you look at my hand for so long?" he asked. You weren't sure?"

"I was sure, but I saw something else. When you go on your honeymoon, do not take a plane. Take the bus, take the train or drive, but do not take a plane."

The wedding was great. Everybody enjoyed it. Everybody was happy. Harry and Kathy received many presents. The best one was from Kathy's parents – a trip to an exotic place. It was a stay in an all-inclusive resort, and of course they paid for the plane tickets too.

Harry and Kathy were in a taxi. They were heading to the airport. Harry thought about what the gypsy had said, and he was scared to death.

"Kathy, Harry said suddenly. I don't want to take a plane. I'm scared. I'm so sorry. I know how you've been looking forward to the trip. But I can't get on a plane."

"You never told me you were scared to take a plane, Kathy said. "It's ok, honey. Don't worry about it. We'll go elsewhere, and we'll drive there."

Kathy told the taxi driver to take them back home. She didn't ask Harry any questions. She was so understanding. The gypsy was right. She really was the one for him.

In the evening Harry and Kathy watched the news. Suddenly they opened their eyes wide in horror. They saw the airport and a burning plane.

"The plane went down just a few seconds after it took off – an engine failure …," the reporter was saying. They hugged each other. Kathy was crying. They knew. It was their plane.

The next day Harry drove to the rest stop.

"I've come to thank you," he said to the gypsy. You saved my life and Kathy's life too. But how did you know about the plane? That's what I want to know.

Arana looked at him. "I don't remember saying anything about a plane," she said. "Don't take everything so seriously. I've got no special power. I'm here to entertain people. That's all."

I. **Complete the sentences with the words from the box below.**

| failure | propose | dilemma | bluffing |
| understanding | blushed | ~~gloomy~~ | irritated |

1. Harry was depressed. He was in a _gloomy_ mood.

2. Harry thought the gypsy was lying to get some money from him. He thought she was _____.

3. Harry became angry. He didn't like the way the gypsy spoke to him. He was _____.

4. The gypsy thought Harry gave her too much money. Her face went red. She _____.

5. Harry couldn't decide if he should start a business with his brother or not. He had a _____.

6. Harry was going to ask Kathy to marry him. He was going to _____ to her.

7. Kathy was a very sympathetic and kind woman. She was _____.

8. When an engine stops working when it is not supposed to, we call it an engine _____.

II. **Choose two words from the box on the previous page and write a short paragraph using them.**

_____
_____
_____
_____

III. **Complete the sentences with the expressions from the box below.**

| idea struck him | pros and cons |
| made your day | telling fortunes |

1. The gypsy hoped Harry would feel good because of what she had said. She said, "I hope I _____."

2. Harry was considering the positive and the negative things. He was considering the _____.

3. An idea suddenly came to Harry's mind. An _____.

4. The gypsy was telling people about their future. She was _____.

IV. **Choose two expressions from the box above and write a short paragraph using these expressions.**

_____
_____
_____
_____

V. Answer the questions in full sentences.

1. Where was Harry going at the beginning of the story?
2. Why was he in a gloomy mood?
3. What did the gypsy tell him?
4. Why did Harry go see the gypsy?
5. What did she tell him?
6. Why did Harry go see her for the second time?
7. What did she tell him?
8. Why did Harry go see her for the third time?
9. What did she tell him?

VI. Oral Summary

Retell the story in a few sentences.

VII. Written Summary

Write a few sentences to summarize the story.

_____
_____
_____
_____
_____
_____
_____
_____

THE FIRE FIGHTER

A deafening bell began to ring. The sound was unbearable as it pealed throughout the school hallways.

"Fire! Fire!" somebody yelled. The students ran out of the classrooms. There was chaos as the students ran down the stairs trying to get out of the building as fast as they could.

Brent Bradley was slowly walking along the wall of the hallway trying to avoid being knocked down by one of his frightened schoolmates.

"Nutcases, he thought to himself – a false alarm. How many times had it happened recently? Like every second week? It didn't matter how many times they practiced fire drills, there had always been complete mayhem.

Some of the students were really scared. Some pretended excitement. Brent Bradley just didn't care. He had more important things on his mind.

Brent was a bad boy, and he had many problems. But there were two major issues at the top of his list. The first and most important issue was that the prom was coming up. He had asked Alice, a classmate who he really liked, to go with him. She was taking her time, and hadn't given him an answer yet. She had told him she might go with somebody better than him. The second thing was that he was facing expulsion from school for inappropriate behavior. He had had an argument with a teacher. He had often argued with teachers, but this time it was much more serious. Many teachers would be very happy if he were to be expelled. Then his first issue wouldn't be an issue anymore because he wouldn't be able to go to the prom anyway.

Brent waited quietly until everybody left the building. Then he went to the bathroom and lit a cigarette. Everything was quiet and peaceful. Finally he had time to think.

Ten minutes later Brent walked out of the building and joined the crowd outside. Nobody had noticed his absence.

There was a man from the fire department in the school yard. He was talking about all the precautions that had to be taken to prevent fire.

"Do not use or play with an open fire in the building," he said. "And if you smoke, make sure the cigarette is completely put out."

"The students are not allowed to smoke in the building," the teacher said. "Actually nobody is allowed to smoke inside. It's a smoke free building."

"That's perfect," the man said. He looked genuinely happy.

"Fire!" somebody yelled. Everybody laughed. They thought it was a joke. But they didn't laugh for long. As they looked at the building they saw flames coming from a window on the third floor. It was the bathroom window.

Everybody looked at the firefighter. He was the one who was supposed to know what to do. And he did, but somebody was quicker than him. A boy was running very quickly towards the building. It was Brent.

"Don't go in," the firefighter called to him. "Come back! I'm going in, not you." But Brent didn't stop and didn't come back. The fire fighter ran after him. Everybody else stayed outside and waited. Brent and the firefighter disappeared into the building.

Brent ran up the stairs. He reached the hallway on the third floor in less than a minute. He ran to the fire extinguisher, pulled it off the wall, and then ran to the bathroom. He opened the door. The fire had spread, and there was a lot of smoke. It was the first time he had used a fire extinguisher, but somehow he managed to get it to work.

The firefighter joined him, and they put out the fire together. Brent became a hero. The fire department awarded him a medal, Alice agreed to go with him to the prom, and they forgot about expelling him from school. The only person who still wanted him to be expelled was Ms. Sutherland. She was the teacher who he argued with the most, and who he had insulted a few days earlier. But nobody paid attention to her.

The years went by, and the staff at the school did not forget Brent. They always mentioned him as a hero when they talked about fire precautions and fire fighting.

"Once, there was a student at our school who didn't hesitate to risk his life to prevent damage to his beloved school," they always said.

"Right," said Ms. Sutherland sarcastically when she heard these kinds of comments. "The boy was a cheater. He knew how to pull the wool over people's eyes."

One Saturday night the people in town were awakened by the sound of sirens. An apartment building was on fire. Firefighters arrived at the scene and started their routine. They knew what to do. They had been trained to fight fires. Bystanders hovered outside watching them.

"Go home," the firefighters yelled at them. "It's not some show to watch. Let us do our job."

Some of the firefighters ran into the building and started to evacuate people from the building. One of them was a tall well-built man. He was breaking doors and checking to see if anybody was inside the apartments. It seemed that everybody had escaped from the building. Then he heard a soft voice in the distance.

"Please help me," a woman's voice called. It was coming from an apartment at the end of the hallway. He ran to the door where he thought the voice was coming from. He broke the door with his axe and walked into the apartment. A woman was lying on the bed. He recognized her right away.

"Ms. Sutherland," he said. "Can you walk? I'll get you out of here."

"Bradley?!" she said, "The bad boy, the cheater!"

"Yes, it's me. We could chat later if you want, but now come with me."

She couldn't walk, so he picked her up and carried her out of the apartment. She wanted to say something, but she couldn't. She was coughing. They were on the fifth floor. Brent began to run down the stairs with her. When they were on the second floor, she finally managed to say something.

"Fluffy," she said quietly. "You've got to save Fluffy."

"Who the hell is Fluffy?" Brent asked.

"Fluffy is my cat. She's in the apartment. Please, save her."

Brent ran down the stairs and out of the building. He gave Ms. Sutherland to the paramedics waiting outside, and then ran back to the building.

"Wait!" his boss called to him. "Don't go in. Come back. It's too dangerous."

But Brent didn't hear him. He was already running up the stairs. He was on a mission.

It was more difficult now. The fire had spread throughout the building. Brent reached the apartment with difficulty. He looked for the cat, but he didn't see her anywhere. Brent remembered the cat he used to have when he was a boy. She would hide under the bed, he thought. He looked under the bed in the bedroom. She wasn't there. Then he looked under the couch in the living room. There she was! He picked her up. He wanted to get out of the building as fast as possible, but now he was in big trouble. The fire had spread everywhere. There was no safe way out.

Brent quickly considered his options. Then he made a decision. He put the cat under his fireproof jacket and ran.

Avoiding the flames was not always possible, so at times he had to run through them.

It took him a long time. Everybody outside thought he was dead. Suddenly he emerged from the building and collapsed on the ground. The paramedics ran to him. They gave him first aid and took him to the hospital.

Brent had serious injuries. His body was badly burnt, and he was in a coma. He became famous overnight. He became a national hero. Everybody wanted to know about the man who had risked his life to save a cat. Everybody waited for him to wake up. And three days later he did.

Now a lot of people wanted to speak to him. After his family, the first person who visited him was Ms. Sutherland.

"Ms. Sutherland!" Brent called when he saw her. "How is Fluffy? Did she survive?"

Ms. Sutherland laughed. "You almost died and you care about a cat? Yes, she survived. She wasn't even hurt. You protected her well. Cats have nine lives. Did you know that?"

"I'm glad to hear that," Brent said. "I wanted to do the right thing for once. I've done many bad things. You were right about me, and everybody else was wrong."

Ms. Sutherland smiled. "What are you talking about?"

"You know what I'm talking about – the fire at our school. You were right. I …"

"Shh, do not say a word." Ms Sutherland put a finger to her lips. "I've come to say thank you for saving my life and Fluffy's life. I think you've grown into an incredibly brave man. I *was* wrong about you."

Journalists were standing outside the hospital as Ms. Sutherland came out. One of them walked up to her.

"Ms. Sutherland," she said. "Do you have a minute? I'd like to ask you a question."

"Fire away," Ms. Sutherland said.

"I've done some research, and I understand that ten years ago you wanted Brent Bradley to be expelled from school. Actually you were the only one who wanted that. You said that he had set a fire in the school bathroom while he was smoking there. He is the same man who saved your life and your cat's life. What have you got to say about that?"

"Only that I was wrong," Ms. Sutherland said. "Brent Bradley is the most courageous man I've ever known. And he's also an honest man."

I. **Complete the sentences with the words from the box below.**

pealed	mission	~~deafening~~	precautions
hovered	mayhem	emerged	unbearable

1. The sound of the bell was very loud. It was a _deafening_ sound.

2. The sound of the bell was so loud that it was almost _____.

3. As the bell _____ throughout the school hallways, the students started to run out of the building.

4. It was a confusing situation. Some students were frightened. It was complete _____.

5. The firefighter talked about the things that should prevent a fire. He talked about _____.

6. People stood and watched the firefighters working. They _____ outside watching them.

7. Brent had something on his mind. He knew what to do. He was on a _____.

8. Everybody thought Brent was dead. But suddenly he _____ from the building.

II. Choose two words from the box on the previous page and write a short paragraph using them.

_____
_____
_____
_____

III. Complete the sentences with the expressions from the box below.

| facing expulsion | paid attention |
| fire away | fire drills |

1. The students practiced what to do in case of a fire. They practiced _____.

2. They wanted to expel Brent from the school. He was _____.

3. Nobody cared what Ms. Sutherland was saying. Nobody _____ to her.

4. The journalist wanted to ask Ms. Sutherland a question. She was ready. She said, "_____."

IV. Choose two expressions from the box above and write a short paragraph using these expressions.

_____
_____
_____
_____

V. Answer the questions in full sentences.

1. Why was Brent calm when he heard the fire alarm?
2. What did Brent do when everybody ran out?
3. Who set the fire in the bathroom? How did he do it?
4. Why did Brent become a hero?
5. Why did Ms. Sutherland want Brent to be expelled?
6. What did Brent become?
7. Who was Fluffy?
8. What happened years later in Brent's life?
9. What did Ms. Sutherland say about Brent in the end?

VI. Summary

Retell the story in a few sentences.

VII. Written Summary

Write a few sentences to summarize the story.

_____
_____
_____
_____
_____
_____
_____
_____

SOOTIE

It was Kevin's birthday, and he was very excited. He had just turned six, and he was finally a big boy. In a few months he was going to start school. But that was not the only reason why he was so excited. Daddy had promised him a special gift for his sixth birthday. What could it be? he wondered. He was very impatient. He couldn't wait.

Finally the time arrived. Everything was ready. His family was there, his friends were there, and a big cake with six candles was there. His birthday party finally began.

"Come on Kevin," his father said smiling. "Close your eyes, make a wish and blow out the candles."

Kevin closed his eyes and wished for something. He didn't tell anybody what it was. He had wished for a cat – a black cat. He had wanted a black cat ever since he could remember. But his parents had always told him that having a cat was a big responsibility, and he was too small to take care of one. Today he was a big boy, so maybe ... He believed that one day his wish would come true.

Kevin got many presents – some books, two toy cars, a train set, a pair of pajamas, three t-shirts and some socks.

But where was the special surprise present from Daddy? He was disappointed.

Suddenly the doorbell rang. Who could it be? Everybody in his family was there. All the friends he had invited were there.

"Go and answer the door," his father said. "Maybe you've forgotten to invite somebody, and he or she has come anyway."

Kevin got up and went to answer the door. He opened the door. There was a middle aged woman at the door. Kevin had never seen her before. "I'll get my parents," Kevin said.

"Wait," the woman said. "I've got something for you. Isn't it your birthday today?"

"It is," Kevin said. "But I don't know you. I'm not allowed to talk to strangers."

The woman smiled. "You're a smart boy, but you can talk to me. I'm from the animal shelter, and I have a present for you. What do you think about that?"

She reached into a bag and took out a little black kitten.

"Wow," Kevin said. "So it really worked. It's unbelievable. I'm so happy. That's all I wanted for my birthday."

"Take good care of him, Kevin," she said. She handed him the kitten, turned around, and before he could say thank you, she was gone.

Kevin ran back into the room with his kitten. "Thank you so much, Daddy. Thank you, Mom," he said. He didn't care about the other presents. He even forgot about his friends. He started to play with the kitten. "I'll call him Sootie," he said, "Because he's black like soot."

And then it happened. Kevin would never forget it. Everybody was staring at him. His face and hands turned red, and he started to sneeze and couldn't stop.

"Put the kitten down, Kevin," his mother said. "There's something wrong with him. "I didn't like the idea of giving him a kitten," she said to her husband.

"I don't think there is anything wrong with the kitten," his father said. "I think Kevin is allergic to cats. That's all."

The doctor confirmed what his father had thought. Kevin was allergic to cats. "It's nothing serious," the doctor said. Many people are allergic to animals. Just keep him away from cats. That's all."

They found the kitten another home. "It's so unfair," Kevin cried. "I wanted him so much. I'm so sad. It was my wish, and it didn't come true. I don't believe in anything anymore."

His parents tried to comfort him, but it didn't work. His little heart was broken, and the memory of it stayed with him for years to come.

Kevin grew up. The trauma from his childhood faded away. He knew he couldn't go near a cat, but it was not so painful anymore. He had other interests in his life. The episode seemed to be forgotten. But was it?

The years went by. Kevin became a smart young man. He was an engineer, and his job was to design planes. He almost never thought about what had happened at his birthday party years ago. And when he did, he thought it was kind of funny. He and his friends had a good laugh when he told them about it.

It would have been the end of the story, but something was about to happen – something that would change Kevin's life forever.

One day Kevin received a letter from Cairo, Egypt. It was a registered letter, and it looked important. He was surprised because he didn't know anybody in Egypt. He opened the envelope and took out the letter. It was a letter from a lawyer. He started to read. As he was reading the expression on his face changed from surprised to astonished. A great-uncle he had never met had died in Cairo last week and had left him all his personal possessions. The funny thing was he didn't even know he had had a great-uncle who lived in Egypt.

I can use some of the money to pay off my mortgage, he thought. How nice of him!

Kevin took a one-week vacation and traveled to Cairo. As he found himself sitting in the lawyer's office he still couldn't believe it was true.

Mr. Gamal, his great-uncle's lawyer, was a very polite man. He spoke slowly with an accent, but his English was almost perfect.

"First of all," Mr. Gamal started. "Please accept my condolences on the loss of your great-uncle Hubert. He really was a great man. He spoke a lot about you before he died."

"Thank you for your sympathy," Kevin said. He was certainly sorry that his great-uncle Hubert had died, but a week ago he hadn't even known he existed. So it was difficult to feel pain. He felt a little bit ashamed because he secretly wished that his great-uncle had left him a large amount of money.

"Your great-uncle wanted me to be his executor," Mr. Gamal continued. "He left all his assets to you. I've looked into his financial situation and his business and personal deals …"

Come on, say it, Kevin thought. How much is it?

"I've found out that he had $2,001,055 dollars in his accounts …"

Kevin's jaw dropped. He couldn't speak – more than two million? It was much more than he had hoped for.

"But," Mr. Gamal said. "Some of his business partners have come forward claiming he owned them money. After paying off all his debts there's only $777 left. But I have good news for you. Your great-uncle Hubert left you something special, something valuable – something that can't be easily bought."

Kevin hardly listened. He was so disappointed. Mr. Gamal left the room and came back with a cage in his hand. "He left you this," he said triumphantly.

"What is it?" Kevin asked.

"It's Ramses," Mr. Gamal said. "He belongs to the Egyptian nobility." Mr. Gamal opened the cage, and a black cat walked out of it.

Kevin's nose started to itch. He sneezed.

"So what do you say?" Mr. Gamal asked smiling.

"I don't want the cat," Kevin said loudly. "I shouldn't have come here. I made a mistake."

"But you don't understand," Mr. Gamal said. "It's not an ordinary cat. It's a Mau. It's a rare breed. Ramses is very intelligent. He can do things that ordinary pets can't."

"*You* don't understand," Kevin shouted. "I *don't* want a cat. I'm allergic to cats."

"Think about it," Mr. Gamal said. "It was your great-uncle's wish. It was very important to him. You could always sell Ramses later if he should cause you any problems. You could easily sell him for $10,000."

Ten thousand dollars is a lot of money, Kevin thought. "OK," he finally said. I'll keep him." But he thought, I'll sell him as fast as I can.

Kevin signed all the legal documents the lawyer had prepared for him and left for the airport. He was carrying the cage with Ramses inside – Egyptian nobility as Mr. Gamal had called him. His flight was in three hours. At least it was supposed to be in three hours. But when he got to the airport, a big surprise was waiting for him. Due to a strike all the flights were cancelled. Kevin had to spend at least one night in Cairo. All the hotels near the airport were full. Kevin waited patiently for a taxi.

Two hours later he finally got into a taxi. "Take me to the nearest hotel, please," he told the taxi driver. They tried three hotels, but all of them were full.

"You could stay in my aunt's house for a night if you don't mind," the taxi driver said. "It's not as comfortable as a hotel, but she has an extra room with a bed and a bathroom." Kevin didn't want to, but after trying two other hotels with the same result, he finally said "yes."

The taxi driver was right. The room was not comfortable. But Kevin was very tired. He put the cage with the cat as far from the bed as he could and went to sleep. A dream came shortly after he closed his eyes. He dreamed about pharaohs, cats and snakes. Why were there snakes in his dream?

Suddenly Kevin woke up. He heard a noise, but he didn't know what it was. He couldn't place it. Then he saw it. He had seen many horror movies. He had seen all the Indiana Jones movies. But he could never have imagined he would have to live through this. His worst nightmare had just come true. He was looking into a snake's eyes. It was a big Egyptian cobra. It was on his bed hissing and ready to attack. Kevin was frozen in fear. He couldn't move. The snake had completely hypnotized him. This is the end, Kevin thought. I'm going to die here far from my home. And that's because I was greedy. I shouldn't have wanted the money that didn't belong to me in the first place.

But it wasn't the end. There was another noise in the far corner of the room. Ramses had torn the cage wires to pieces and gotten out of the cage. Without hesitation he jumped on the bed and attacked the snake. He bit its tail and pulled it off the bed. The snake forgot about Kevin. It concentrated on its new enemy. Kevin will never forget the ferocious fight he witnessed. He would have never thought it was possible – a cat killing a cobra.

Ramses walked up to Kevin and looked at him victoriously.

It was difficult to smile after what had just happened, but Kevin smiled at him. "I'm supposed to say 'thank you', aren't I?" Kevin said. "Do you understand English?"

Ramses kept looking at Kevin with his beautiful green eyes.

"Yes, I think you do. So thank you for saving my life. I'll never forget it." He took the cat in his hands and petted him. Ramses was bleeding from several cuts. The cobra hadn't hurt him. He had cut himself as he was getting out of the cage through the wires. Kevin took a clean towel and wiped off the blood. As he was tending to him, he realized he hadn't sneezed. His skin hadn't turned red. Had his allergy disappeared? It certainly looked like it.

"I'll tell you what, pal, Kevin said. "I'll keep you. Mr. Gamal was right about you. You can certainly do things other pets can't. You've just shown me that. I'll take care of you. You'll be my cat and my friend forever. But there's one condition. You'll live in America with me. We don't believe in aristocracy in America. So I won't call you Ramses if you don't mind. I'll call you Sootie. What do you say to that?"

Ramses or Sootie now looked at Kevin and purred. He didn't mind. Kevin's childhood dream had just come true.

I. Complete the sentences with the words from the box below.

strangers	astonished	assets	staring
greedy	~~responsibility~~	disappointed	ashamed

1. Kevin's parents thought that taking care of a cat was not easy. They thought it was a big _responsibility_ .

2. Kevin expected a surprise present. He got many things, but nothing exciting. He was _____ .

3. Kevin was not allowed to talk to people he didn't know. He was not allowed to talk to _____ .

4. Everybody was looking at Kevin for a long time. They were _____ at him.

5. As Kevin read the letter, he was very surprised. He was _____ .

6. He felt very bad because his great-uncle had died, and he had thought about his money. He felt _____ .

7. Kevin inherited everything his great-uncle had. He inherited all his _____ .

8. Kevin thought he wanted to get rich, and he didn't deserve it. He thought he was too _____ .

II. **Choose two words from the box on the previous page and write a short paragraph using them.**

_____
_____
_____
_____

III. **Complete the sentences with the expressions from the box below.**

faded away	heart was broken
tending to him	jaw dropped

1. Kevin was extremely unhappy and disappointed. His little _____.

2. Kevin's trauma from his childhood went away slowly. It _____.

3. Kevin couldn't believe what he had just heard. He was very surprised. His _____.

4. Kevin was wiping off Ramses's blood with a clean towel. He was _____.

IV. **Choose two expressions from the box above and write a short paragraph using these expressions.**

_____
_____
_____
_____

V. Answer the questions in full sentences.

1. Why was Kevin excited at the beginning of the story?
2. What was the surprise present?
3. What happened at his birthday party?
4. How did he cope with the trauma from his childhood?
5. What happened later in Kevin's life?
6. Why did he feel ashamed about his inheritance?
7. Why was he disappointed when he found out more?
8. Why did he reluctantly accept his inheritance?
9. Why did he decide to keep Ramses in the end?

VI. Oral Summary

Retell the story in a few sentences.

VII. Written Summary

Write a few sentences to summarize the story.

_____
_____
_____
_____
_____
_____
_____
_____

THE ENCHANTED FOREST I

It was Friday afternoon and Jerry April was slowly driving his jeep through a village. He was just passing through. The name of the village was Old Raisin. He was going to meet his old school buddies, and he was not in a hurry. The weather was beautiful. Spring had definitely arrived. He looked at the old houses and the church. He knew the village very well. Then his eyes wandered to the forest beyond the village. Since he was a little boy he had been wondering what was in that forest. People called it the enchanted forest. They said that witches lived there. And they said that there was a hole somewhere deep in the forest. If you fell in the hole you would emerge in another century. Did Jerry believe it? – of course not. It was ridiculous – just another fake story to attract tourists to a godforsaken place. But he had to admit that the village had some allure because of the story. He decided that one day he would go into the forest and explore it. Then he would tell everybody that it was only a fairy tale for children. He couldn't have guessed that it would be sooner than he had thought.

Jerry was a journalist and worked for an important newspaper. On Monday, Mr. Samuel Harper, the editor, called him. He wanted to see Jerry in his office.

"Jerry," Mr. Samuel Harper said. "I've got something for you. Have you ever heard of Old Raisin? It's a small village about 90 miles away from here."

"You're joking, right Sam?" Jerry said. "It's funny you should ask me that. I was thinking about that village as I drove through it last Friday."

"That's good," Mr. Harper said, "Because you're going there. People have been talking about Old Raisin recently. They're saying weird things about that village. There's a legend attached to it. They call the legend Old Raisin's Hole. The legend has even gotten international attention."

"You're pulling my leg, Sam," Jerry said. "You can't be serious."

"I'm damn serious, Jerry. You have three days. Try to dig something up or maybe make something up. You'd better write a good story."

"I'm sorry, Sam," Jerry said. "But I thought there were more important things around the world than some fake legends and fairy tales for children, and I …"

"Well, Jerry, you were wrong," said Mr. Harper. "That's why I'm the editor, and you're not. Got it?"

"Yes, sir," Jerry said. There was no point in arguing with Sam. He had already made up his mind.

So the next day Jerry was back in Old Raisin again. He had passed through the village many times before, but he had never thought of stopping and exploring it – except last Friday. Well, now was the time to do it. He had no other choice.

Jerry went to the local bar. It was the best place to start his research – at least he thought so. A few old men were sitting there, drinking beer and talking. Jerry knew what to do. He bought them a drink and started a casual conversation. After a little while he decided to ask about the legend.

"I hear there is an interesting legend attached to your village," Jerry started.

The men looked at him. They seemed to get serious.

"You're right," one of them said. "There are witches here. My wife is one of them."

"I have a witch at home too," another one said. They all burst into laughter and couldn't stop. It was time for Jerry to go.

He was walking through the village thinking about what to do next. He saw two old women sitting outside a house. I'll just give it another try, he thought. But when he asked them they got angry. "I wish people would stop asking about nonsense," one of them said. "We had a bus of Japanese tourists here last month because of it. It's getting crazier and crazier every day."

Frustrated Jerry was leaving when somebody called to him. "Wait!"

He turned around. An old man was trying to catch up with him.

"I heard you asking about our village in the pub," the man said. "I recognized you. You're Jerry April. Sometimes I read your articles. You seem to be a reasonable man. I felt sorry for you. There's something I want you to know. A long time ago a young woman lived here. Her name was Erika. Some people said she was a witch. Some said she was just crazy. She went into the forest one day and never came back. The whole village searched for her for months, but they couldn't find her. The rumor about witches started then. Some people think she still lives somewhere in the forest. But if you believe a hole to another century exists, I can't help you." He turned around and walked away.

"Thanks," Jerry called after him. The man just raised his hand and waved. Soon he was out of sight.

Now what? Jerry thought. Jerry had some flaws, but giving up easily was not one of them. He started to walk. Before he fully realized where he was going, he found himself in the forest. He kept walking. There were hiking trails, but they soon disappeared. Jerry was deep in the forest. Something made him walk deeper and deeper into the forest.

The weather changed without warning. The wind started to blow. There was lightning, and the forest went dark. Jerry decided to go back to the village, but he was disoriented. He realized he didn't know which direction to turn. He pulled out his phone – no Internet, no signal. Now what? Fate decided for him. Suddenly he heard a loud cracking sound, and then everything went black.

"Wake up, Jerry." Somebody was talking to him. He opened his eyes. He was lying on a bed in a shack. His head hurt. An old woman was looking at him.

"You're awake, at last," she said and smiled. It was a lot of work for me to bring you here. You were very lucky that I found you."

"How come you know my name?" Jerry asked.

"Because I'm a witch, and I know black magic. And I'm going to put you in an oven and eat you." She started to laugh. "I looked through your pockets. I saw your driver's license."

"What happened to me?" Jerry asked.

"You were hit on the head by a falling branch," the woman said. "You'll be alright."

"Are you a doctor?" Jerry asked.

"No, but I know more about medicine than most doctors," the woman said. "I'm a medicine woman. I've been studying nature for forty years."

"You must be Erika – the lost witch."

"They decided I was a witch because I was different – smarter and prettier than them. I ran into the forest before they could harm me. I've built this little house, and I've been living here in harmony with nature for many years."

"Aren't you lonely sometimes?" Jerry asked.

"I got used to being alone. I'm happy here. But what are *you* doing here?"

"I went hiking, and I got lost," Jerry lied.

"Right," Erika smiled. "I saw your press badge. Tell your boss that you found the witch. And she didn't kill you. She let you go."

Jerry got up and looked out the window. The sun was shining. The birds were singing. He must have slept for a long time.

"I'll show you the way out," she said.

They walked for a long time. Finally they reached a crossroads.

"If you go to the right, you'll get to Old Raisin in a few hours," Erika said, "And you can go back to your boring life. If you go to the left, you might find something exciting. But it's dangerous, and you might die. Now it's up to you."

Jerry thanked Erika and went to the right. He certainly didn't want to die. Erika hid behind a tree and watched him leaving. Jerry suddenly stopped, turned around and went back to the crossroads. He had changed his mind. He had chosen excitement over boredom.

"Yes!" Erika said to herself. "Yes! He's the right man. I've been waiting for him."

Jerry didn't want to go back to the village – not just yet. He took his job very seriously, and he was no coward. He wanted to know what Erika meant when she said it was a dangerous road. He was about to find out.

He walked up a hill for some time. He reached the top and looked down into a little valley. On the other side of the valley he saw something that made his blood run cold. There was a rock. It looked like a woman's face. With a little imagination he was able to discern her hair, eyes, nose, and … and mouth. It looked like an open mouth – a hole. Was that the hole he had heard about? He decided to find out.

He started to descend into the valley. There were no trails, so it took him a long time. Finally he reached the rock. The hole that looked like an open mouth from a distance was a cave. He took a flashlight out of his backpack and walked into the cave. The cave was about ten feet wide. He took a few steps forward and reached a wall. It was just about thirty feet deep. Jerry was disappointed. There was nothing there. But he didn't want to give up. He started to inspect the walls inch by inch –

nothing. He was about to give up when he noticed some lines on the wall. It was writing – an inscription. It read:

Tempus significat nihil.

I. **Complete the sentences with the words from the box below.**

allure	casual	discern	rumor
flaws	~~enchanted~~	shack	weird

1. The forest was full of magic. It was an _enchanted_ forest.

2. The forest was mysterious and exciting. It had some _____.

3. People talked about witches and a hole through which you could get to another century. It was _____.

4. Jerry talked about things which were not important. He started _____ conversation.

5. The _____ about witches in the forest started after Erika disappeared and people couldn't find her.

6. Jerry was not a perfect man. He had many _____, but giving up was not one of them.

7. Erika lived in a little house that she had built for herself. She lived in a little _____.

8. Jerry was far from the rock, but with a little imagination he could _____ a woman's face.

II. Choose two words from the box on the previous page and write a short paragraph using them.

_____
_____
_____
_____

III. Complete the sentences with the expressions from the box below.

fairy tales	pulling my leg
his blood run cold	godforsaken place

1. Jerry thought there was nothing attractive about the village. He thought it was a _____.

2. Jerry didn't believe in witches. He believed witches were only in _____.

3. Jerry thought his boss was joking about the magic forest. He said, "You're _____."

4. The thing that Jerry saw was very frightening. It made _____.

IV. Choose two expressions from the box above and write a short paragraph using these expressions.

_____
_____
_____
_____

V. Answer the questions in full sentences.

1. Where was Jerry driving at the beginning of the story?
2. Why did the village he drove through have some allure?
3. What did his boss tell him to do?
4. What did Jerry think about the magic forest?
5. What did the people in the village tell him about it?
6. What happened to Jerry in the forest?
7. Who helped Jerry?
8. What did Erika tell Jerry?
9. What did Jerry find at the end?

VI. Oral Summary

Retell the story in a few sentences.

VII. Written Summary

Write a few sentences to summarize the story.

THE ENCHANTED FOREST II

It was Latin. He didn't speak or read Latin, but it was not difficult to understand.

Time means nothing.

Jerry wanted to take a closer look. He took two more steps towards the wall. Suddenly the ground swallowed him up. He was sliding into darkness. He closed his eyes to protect them. It was strange, but it seemed to him he had been sliding in slow motion for a long time before he hit the ground. He opened his eyes. He was in a cave. For an instant he thought it was the same cave, but it was not possible. He was confused. Where was the tunnel he had just come out of? He didn't see it anywhere. He got up and tried to move. He was not hurt. He walked out of the cave. It was not the same cave. It couldn't have been. The forest around him looked different, and the inscription on the wall was not there. But the woman's face on the rock was there – very strange.

Jerry decided to explore the forest around him. He checked his phone. It was broken. He must have broken it when he fell into the hole. He decided that the cave would be his landmark. He walked into the valley, and then into the forest leaving the rock with the cave behind him. He could always come back and try a different direction.

After walking for almost four hours he came out of the forest. He saw small houses in the distance – a village, but what a village! He saw thatched houses and people wearing strange clothes. It looked like a village from the 17th century. Are they making a movie there? he thought. He didn't see a film crew or any movie making equipment. Wait a minute. Is it possible that the legend about the hole is true? No, no way. I must be dreaming, he thought. Since he was a little boy, he had always had dreams that seemed so real. He decided to play along and explore the village.

He noticed that some men were wearing long coats and hats. He needed a coat and a hat to look like them. He didn't want anybody to notice him. He waited until it got dark. Something was happening. Many villagers were walking towards a little hill beyond the village. Soon the village was almost empty. Now was the time. He quickly walked down to the village. Nobody noticed him. He walked into a house. He found a long dirty coat and a big hat. He put them on and joined the crowd walking up the hill. When they got to the top, he understood. He had read about it. He had seen it in movies. He would have never guessed that he would witness it for real. Was it real or just a dream? He was going to witness the burning of a so-called witch. A woman was tied to a post.

People were talking excitedly. It seemed they were looking forward to it. It was a horrible time, he thought. He was happy he lived in a different century.

Suddenly there was silence. Somebody started to talk, and everybody listened. Jerry elbowed his way closer to see better.

"Lisa May," an important-looking man was saying. "You were convicted of witchcraft, and you're going to be burned at the stake. Now you have one last chance to say something before you die."

Jerry looked at the woman. What he saw surprised him. She was young and very pretty. He had a different image of witches in his head. In the fairy tales his mother used to tell him, the witch was always old and ugly. They wanted to kill this young beautiful girl for nothing? Jerry must do something quickly, but what? All of a sudden an idea came to him.

The woman was very brave. She didn't cry or beg. She looked at the man with her piercing eyes. "Judge Lord," she said. "You're right. I'm a fierce cruel witch. Look into my eyes. I'm casting a terrible spell on you."

A shiny red spot appeared on Judge Lord's face. It moved to his eye. He screamed and fell to the ground.

"Kill the witch!" people shouted. A man with an ax stepped forward. The woman looked at him. Again a shiny red spot appeared on his eye. The man screamed and fell to the ground. The others didn't need to see more. They ran away. Only Jerry stayed. He walked to the stake and untied the woman.

"Come with me, quickly!" he said.

The woman hesitated. "Who are you?" she asked.

"Somebody who wants to help you. Come with me, or they'll kill you."

They ran as fast as they could. Jerry was leading the way. Soon they were in the forest. But they didn't stop running. After running for two hours, they were exhausted and finally stopped. They fell to the ground breathing heavily.

"Why are you doing this?" Lisa asked. "And who the hell are you?"

"I came here from another century. I mean the 21st century," Jerry said. "I fell into the hole that connects your century with my century. But I think that you're not real, and everything is only a dream, and I'll wake up soon."

She smiled. "I know who you are."

"You do?" Jerry was surprised.

"Yes, you're a nut. But thank you for saving my life."

They were both smiling now, and for a minute they were relaxed.

"So why did you save me?" Lisa asked after a while.

"Because I don't think you're a witch. We don't believe in witches in my century."

"What do you believe in?"

"We believe that people are generally good although we have some evil people too."

"So what is it like to live in the 21st century?"

"Well, we have big cities with skyscrapers. We have cars, trains and planes so we can travel faster. We have phones and the Internet so we can communicate better."

"Is everything perfect?"

"Of course not, but we don't burn beautiful girls at the stake. We marry them."

Lisa smiled. I don't understand any of the words you mentioned. But I understand what marriage means. Judge Lord wanted to marry me. I refused, and he said I was a witch. But I'm not a witch. I'm just a little smarter than the others. They attribute my cleverness to some kind of witchcraft. Anyway how did you do that?"

"Do what?" Jerry asked.

"How come Judge Lord and the other man fell to the ground when they wanted to hurt me? What was that shiny red spot? I didn't do it. I have no power to cast a spell on anybody. I was just bluffing."

Jerry smiled. He took something out of his pocket and showed it to Lisa.

"What's that?" she asked.

Jerry was beaming with joy now. "It's a laser pointer – one of our greatest inventions. Thank God I kept it in my pocket. We have been warned over and over not to point it at people's eyes because it's dangerous. I've never done it before. So I tried it on them. It looks like they were right. It's dangerous." Jerry pointed the laser pointer at some dead leaves. It didn't take long before the leaves caught fire.

"Wow," Lisa said. If they saw that, they would burn you, not me. I thought you were a nut with all that 21st century talk, but it looks like you're not."

"We've got to go," Jerry said. They might be looking for us. Follow me."

Jerry led Lisa to the cave he had fallen into. He had not noticed it before, but now he saw it clearly. There were stairs in the corner leading up to a hole. He knew what they were – the stairs home.

"Come with me," Jerry said. "You'll be safe. I'll take care of you."

Lisa hesitated. "I don't know," she said.

"They're going to kill you. You'll live in my world."

"OK," Lisa said. She glanced back for the last time. There was somebody coming on a horse. Jerry saw it too.

"Come quickly!" he said. "They're going to get you."

But Lisa didn't move. "Wait," she said. "That's my sister Susan."

Susan stopped and got off the horse. "Come back, Lisa," she said. They're not going to hurt you. People revolted after what happened. They saw it as God's will."

"Come with me," Jerry said. Don't believe those people. They wanted to burn you, remember?"

Lisa hesitated again. "Give me a minute, Sue," she said. Her sister moved away.

Lisa came up to Jerry. "What's your name," she asked. "We were in a hurry, and you forgot tell me your name."

"I'm Jerry."

"Listen, Jerry," she said. "Thanks for everything. I can't leave just like that. I have a mother and a sister here. Give me some time, and I'll come to see you."

"How are you going to find me?" Jerry asked. "It'll be almost impossible for you."

"I'll find you all right," she said and winked at him. "I'm a smart witch. Never forget that."

Other horse riders appeared in the distance. "You have to go," Lisa said. "They might not hurt me, but they might hurt you."

She bent down and picked up a little pebble from the ground. "Keep it to remember me," she said and gave him a kiss.

"It's Jerry April," he said. "I live in a town called Little Ford."

"I'm Lisa May," she said. "I'll come to see you. I always keep my promises. And besides, April is always followed by May, isn't it?" She turned and quickly walked away. She didn't want other people to find the hole in the cave.

Jerry walked up the stairs. Soon he was in the other cave. He was home again. He walked out of the cave.

I. **Complete the sentences with the words from the box below.**

thatched	nut	winked	landmark
stake	~~swallowed~~	fierce	convicted

1. Jerry suddenly fell into a hole. He was sliding somewhere. The ground _swallowed_ him.

2. The cave could be seen from far away. Jerry decided it would be his _____.

3. The houses were made of straw. They were _____ houses.

4. The judge said they had proof that she was a witch. They _____ her of being a witch.

5. Lisa was tied to a post. They were going to burn her at the _____.

6. Lisa told the judge he should be aware of her. She told him she was a _____ witch.

7. Lisa thought Jerry was a crazy person. She thought he was a _____.

8. Lisa closed one of her eyes and opened it again. She _____ at him.

II. Choose two words from the box on the previous page and write a short paragraph using them.

_____
_____
_____
_____

III. Complete the sentences with the expressions from the box below.

piercing eyes	cast a spell
was bluffing	play along

1. Jerry decided to do the same thing as the other people. He decided to _____.

2. Lisa looked at the judge with eyes that showed how much she hated him. She had _____.

3. People thought Lisa was a witch, and she had power to _____ on them.

4. Lisa was not telling the truth. She had no power. She _____.

IV. Choose two expressions from the box above and write a short paragraph using these expressions.

_____
_____
_____
_____

V. Answer the questions in full sentences.

1. What was the writing about?
2. What happened to Jerry in the cave?
3. What did he discover?
4. What were the people about to do?
5. Why was Jerry so surprised?
6. How did Jerry help Lisa?
7. What did Lisa think about Jerry at first?
8. Why did she change her opinion about him?
9. Why didn't Lisa escape with Jerry?

VI. Oral Summary

Retell the story in a few sentences.

VII. Written Summary

Write a few sentences to summarize the story.

_____
_____
_____
_____
_____
_____
_____
_____

THE ENCHANTED FOREST III

"Welcome back, Jerry," a voice behind him said. Jerry almost had a heart attack. He turned around. An old woman was standing behind him.

"Erika? You scared me," Jerry said.

"I've been waiting for you, Erika said. You took a long time. Did you save her?"

"I hope so," Jerry said. "But she didn't want to come with me. How do you know about that?"

"I know many things. I'm a smart witch. Never forget that. I sent you there to save her. I counted on you. You didn't disappoint me. Thank you."

A smart witch, Jerry thought. I've heard that twice today.

Jerry went to Erika's cottage. He was hungry and needed some sleep. He was surprised at how well Erika could cook with the limited resources she had in the forest.

The next morning he was ready to leave.

"Can you do me a favor?" Erika asked.

"Anything you want," Jerry said.

"Do not tell anybody about me. I don't want any publicity. I'm happy here. I just want people to leave me alone."

"Don't worry," Jerry said. "I won't."

Jerry left in a good mood. But he still was not sure if he was dreaming or if everything was real. Had he really visited another century? Who had ever heard of it? – In movies, maybe, but in real life? – Impossible. I'll wake up soon, he thought. I must. But he had no idea that his adventure was far from finished.

Jerry walked for a long time. He hoped he hadn't gotten lost. Suddenly he could smell something. It smelled like smoke. Who could be so stupid as to build a fire in the middle of the forest? Then everything happened so fast that Jerry couldn't escape. He was surrounded by fire. He was trapped. Am I going to die here in a forest fire? he thought. Jerry didn't remember what happened next.

"Jerry?" somebody said.

Jerry opened his eyes. He was in a hospital. His boss Samuel Harper was sitting by his bed.

"Thank God you're awake, Jerry," his boss said.

"What happened to me?" Jerry asked.

"The forest was on fire. When I heard about it, I let the police and the firefighters know. I knew you were there. I'm so sorry, Jerry. I shouldn't have asked you to go there. Thank God they found you. You were right. Who cares about fairy tales and legends? We have more important things to do. You almost died, and it would have been my fault. You'll take a month paid vacation. Then I'm going to need you to work on something else."

"Thanks, Sam," Jerry said. "I'm alright. It was not your fault. You didn't start the fire."

"By the way," Sam asked. "Did you see anything interesting?" Sam couldn't help asking.

"Yes," Jerry said. "I mean no. I'm sorry, Sam. I'm still confused. No, I didn't see anything."

"That's all right," Sam said. "Get well soon, Jerry. Your car will be in the parking lot outside. I'll see to it." Then he was gone.

Jerry tried to get his bearings and think clearly, but it was difficult. He called the nurse and asked her to bring him his personal things. He went through his pockets and his backpack. All his things were there. His phone was broken, but it could have happened when he tried to escape the fire. He didn't find anything that could tell him if his adventure had been real or not. Had everything been only a dream? But it had all seemed so real.

The next morning Jerry woke up late. Now he was well rested and his mind was clear. His adventure must have been a dream. He was sure of it. Now he was glad he hadn't told anybody about it, especially his boss. Sam would have thought he was going crazy, and he could have lost his job. He was not going to think about it anymore.

In the afternoon Jerry was leaving the hospital. He was already outside on the stairs when the nurse caught up with him.

"Mr. April," she said. "Wait. I've found something in your locker. It must have fallen out of your pocket."

Jerry looked at her outstretched hand. She was holding something in it. A shiver ran down his spine. It was a little pebble – the pebble Lisa had given him. *I'll come to see you. I always keep my promises.*

"Mr. April, what's wrong?" she asked. "You are as white as a sheet."

"I'm sorry," Jerry said. "What did you say? I wasn't listening."

"Is this your stone or not? Should I throw it away?"

"It's mine, thank you." Jerry took the pebble from her, put it in his pocket and went to find his car.

Now he thought about his adventure again while he drove home. Had Lisa really given him the pebble? Or had it gotten into his pocket by accident while he was in the forest? He knew the answer.

Summer came and went. Jerry was very busy. He had been working very hard lately. He had been thinking only about his work. The spring adventure never crossed his mind again. He either worked or slept. He didn't have time for anything else.

One October evening, Jerry was relaxing at home. He was watching TV. He was tired and could hardly keep his eyes open. But it was too early to go to sleep. Suddenly the doorbell rang. Jerry got up and went to answer the door. He was upset. He wasn't expecting anybody, and he didn't like being disturbed by surprise visitors. The doorbell rang again, and somebody banged on the door.

"I'm coming," Jerry shouted. "Can't you wait a few seconds?" He opened the door. There were scary looking creatures at his door. "Trick or treat!" they shouted.

Jerry had been so busy lately that he had forgotten about Halloween.

"I'm sorry kids," Jerry said. "No candy this year. What about a few bucks instead?" Jerry went back into the house and brought the children some money. The happy children left, and Jerry went back to his couch.

It was a few minutes past nine when Jerry decided to go to sleep. He had just gotten in bed when his doorbell rang again.

"Oh no," said Jerry. "More kids? It's too late, isn't it?"

He was still talking as he opened the door. "It's not polite to disturb people after nine even if …"

The words froze in his mouth. There weren't any kids asking for candy at his door. A woman stood at his door. He didn't know who she was because she was wearing a mask. She was disguised as a witch.

"I've come to see you, Jerry," she said. "I always keep my promises."

"Lisa?"

"You said you didn't believe in witches in the 21st century, but the first woman I met was an old witch. She told me that my disguise was poor. She gave me this costume and mask. I was very lucky. She knew where you lived."

Jerry laughed. He realized how happy he was to see Lisa. He was happy it had not been only a dream. He pulled her inside. They talked and talked and talked. They had a lot of things to say to each other. They had overcome four hundred years of jet lag. After that they believed there were no more obstacles they couldn't overcome together.

I. Complete the sentences with the words from the box below.

creatures	~~trapped~~	jet lag	confused
disguised	disturbed	obstacles	bucks

1. Jerry was surrounded by fire. There was no way out. He was _trapped_.

2. Jerry didn't know if his adventure was real, or if it had been a dream. He was _____.

3. Jerry didn't want other people to bother him. He didn't want to be _____.

4. There were kids wearing scary masks. They looked like strange _____.

5. Jerry didn't have any candy. He gave the kids some money. He gave them a few _____.

6. Jerry couldn't see the woman's face. She was wearing a mask and a witch's hat. She was _____.

7. Jerry and Lisa overcame the 400-year time difference. They overcame the discomfort of _____.

8. They also overcame everything that had gotten in their way. They overcame all the _____.

II. **Choose two words from the box on the previous page and write a short paragraph using them.**

_____
_____
_____
_____

III. **Complete the sentences with the expressions from the box below.**

see to it	shiver ran down his spine
get his bearings	white as a sheet

1. Sam told Jerry he would arrange for his car to be in the parking lot. He said he would _____.

2. Jerry was confused, but he tried to think clearly about what to do next. He tried to _____.

3. Jerry was very scared. He could feel it in his body. A _____.

4. Jerry's face was very pale. His face was _____.

IV. **Choose two expressions from the box above and write a short paragraph using them.**

_____
_____
_____
_____

V. Answer the questions in full sentences.

1. Who did Jerry meet first in the 21st century?
2. What did Erika ask him?
3. What happened to Jerry in the forest?
4. Who was the first person to visit him in the hospital?
5. What did Sam tell him?
6. Why was Jerry scared after talking to the nurse?
7. Who disturbed Jerry first while he was resting at home?
8. Who disturbed him the second time?
9. How did Jerry feel after he found out who it was?

VI. Oral Summary

Retell the story in a few sentences.

VII. Written Summary

Write a few sentences to summarize the story.

_____
_____
_____
_____
_____
_____
_____

The Texas Rose I

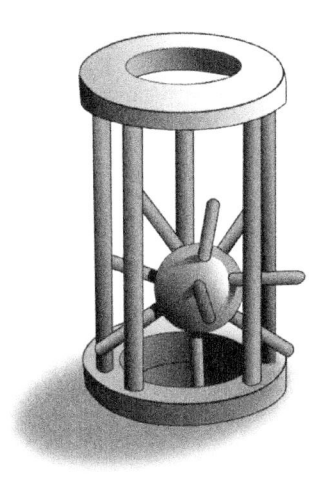

Lilibet had tears in her eyes as she read the letter from her grandfather. Her grandfather Miles had died a week earlier, and he had left her a letter. She had been devastated by his sudden death, and she hadn't been able to find the courage to read it. But he had wanted her to read it, so now she had finally forced herself to do it.

Her grandfather Miles was originally from Czechoslovakia. He had escaped the communist regime in the early fifties and had immigrated to America. He had settled in Dallas, Texas where Lilibet and her entire family now lived.

As she continued reading the pain was almost unbearable, and her tears dropped onto her grandfather's letter.

I've never told you this, but you are my favorite grandchild. I left something back in my home country when I immigrated to America almost forty years ago – something very precious. I want you to have it. It's hidden in a cottage near Prague. Find Karl Kurz. He lives in Prague. He used to be a doctor. He's an old friend of mine. He's going to help you. The cottage belonged to me, and now it's yours. Karl is taking care of it for me. Go to the cottage. Go to the basement. There are tiles on the floor. Lift the tile in the western corner. You'll find the road to eternal happiness there.

Good luck, sweetheart
Your grandfather Miles

"The road to eternal happiness?" Lilibet repeated. My grandfather Miles was a little bit crazy, she thought with a smile. She was thinking about the mischief they had once gotten into together. Well, I guess I'm going to Prague.

Lilibet asked her grandmother and the rest of the family about her grandfather's friend Karl Kurz, but they didn't know anything about him.

"You can't take your grandfather too seriously," they said. "You knew him, didn't you?"

Yes, I knew him, she thought. He was crazy, but he wouldn't send me to Europe without a reason. I'm sure of it.

Lilibet was a woman of action. She was a college student, but she also worked, and she had put some money aside. It's time to break into the piggy bank, she thought.

She called a few private detectives in Prague. One of them spoke decent English and seemed nice. He found Karl Kurz for a reasonable price and gave her his address. Lilibet wrote Karl Kurz a letter, and he answered her. He said her grandfather used to be his best friend, and he was willing to help her with anything she needed.

So one Saturday morning in June 1995, Lilibet found herself at the airport in Prague. She was walking across the terminal when she saw a young man holding a sign with her name on it. She walked up to him.

"I guess that's me," she said pointing at the sign.

"That's great," he said. "I'm Rolf Kurz. My grandfather sent me to pick you up. Come on, you must be tired and hungry. I'm taking you to my grandfather's house where you'll be staying. Don't try to fight with him. He won't let you stay in a hotel."

Lilibet looked at the tall young man. I'm already in love with this country, she thought.

Karl Kurz was a jovial man. He hugged Lilibet and told her she was more than welcome in his house, and she could stay as long as she liked. He asked her many questions about her grandfather and about her. They laughed a lot. They liked each other right from the start.

"You need some rest now," Karl Kurz said. "Rolf will drive you to the cottage tomorrow. It's your cottage now, so you can do whatever you want there. Rolf will wait for you and take you back. Then he'll show you Prague. It's an interesting city, you know."

The next morning Rolf drove a shiny new truck out from the garage.

"My grandfather just bought me this truck for my birthday," he said. We're going to need it. It's a rough road to the cottage. But I'm more than happy to test out my new truck. Let's go!"

Rolf was right. The road was very rough, but his new truck handled it without any problems. One hour later Rolf stopped his truck and pointed at a beautiful mountain cottage. "This is your cottage," he said. "Welcome home. I'll let you go in alone. I'll wait for you here. Take all the time you need." He handed her the key.

Rolf was very polite and Lilibet liked that. "I want you to come with me," she said. "I think I'm going to need you."

The cottage looked impeccably clean. Karl Kurz must be taking good care of it, Lilibet thought. One day I'll come and spend some time here. I like the cottage and the countryside here very much.

But now she had to concentrate on something else. What might my grandfather have left here? She thought. *Something very precious, the road to eternal happiness,* she repeated her grandfather's words.

They went to the basement. It looked like a wine cellar. There was a wooden table surrounded by many chairs and shelves holding wine bottles. My grandfather and his family must have liked wine, she thought. She looked at the floor. There were the tiles just as her grandfather had written.

"Where is the west," she asked Rolf. "Do you know?"

"Let me see," Rolf said. "I think it's that way." He pointed to one of the corners.

Lilibet went to the corner and knocked on one of the tiles. There was a hollow sound. "It must be here," she said.

"What must be here?" Rolf asked.

"My grandfather had a secret hiding place here," she said. "Can you lift this tile?"

"I'll try," Rolf said. He went to get a big screwdriver and started to work. It took some time, but he finally got the tile out. "Here you go," he said. "Come, look." He stepped aside politely.

Lilibet took an iphone out of her pocket and used the flashlight. She pointed the light into the hole. The hole was about two feet deep. There was a wooden box in the hole. She took it out. The box itself was work of art. There was a carved falcon on the lid. Lilibet remembered that her grandfather liked to carve. He must have carved the falcon himself, she thought. There was a combination lock on it. It was not possible to open it without knowing the combination. She certainly didn't want to destroy the box.

"My grandfather didn't give me the combination," she said. "Did he want to play a game with me? Let me see. I need six numbers."

"Six numbers could be somebody's birthday," Rolf said. His eyes were shining with excitement.

Lilibet tried a few birthdays: her grandfather's, her grandmother's, her father's and her mother's, but none of them worked.

"Wait," Rolf shouted suddenly. "What order did you use for the numbers?"

"Well," she said, "The month, the day and the year. That's the order it's supposed to be."

"Yes," Rolf said. "For you, but your grandfather was originally from Czechoslovakia. We always put the day first. Just try it."

Lilibet entered her grandfather's birthday starting with the day. As soon as she entered the last number the lock clicked, and the box opened. "Yes!" they both said at the same time. They were both very excited. She opened the box and looked. There was something strange in the box. She had no idea what it was. She had never seen anything like it before. She took it out. It was a cylindrical cage made of metal. It was about four inches tall and about three inches in diameter. There was a little metallic ball inside the cage with several spikes. Each spike was a different size.

She turned it over. The ball rattled in the cage. But she couldn't get it out.

"Do you have any idea what it is?" she asked Rolf.

Rolf took it from her. He was beaming with joy. "You're asking me if I know what it is?" he said laughing. "Sure I know. Everybody in the Czech Republic knows what it is. It's the most famous puzzle here. It's called the Hedgehog in the Cage. It's from a famous children's book written by Jaroslav Foglar. It's an amazing story."

"Does it have any value?" Lilibet asked.

"Well, you can get a puzzle like this in a toy store here for 450 Czech crowns which is about 20 dollars. This one looks really good. Maybe somebody would be willing to pay 900 Czech crowns for it."

Lilibet couldn't hide her disappointment. She looked at Rolf. But now he had a mischievous smile on his face.

"I'm pulling your leg a little bit," he said and laughed. He looked like a little boy now. "It's not the puzzle itself that has any value. It's the thing hidden in the spiky ball."

"What thing?" she asked.

"That I don't know," he said. The character in the book hid the blueprints for his flying bike there. Unfortunately he was murdered before he could sell his invention to anybody. But it's just a story. It's fiction. It has nothing to do with reality. But I'm almost certain your grandfather put something in there."

"Well, can you get the ball out of the cage?" she asked.

"Well," he said. I think I can. My grandfather told me the story about the Hedgehog in the Cage so many times that I used to know it by heart. You have to know how to turn these spikes in order to get the hedgehog out of his cage."

Rolf must have forgotten this part of the story, because it took him almost two hours to get the ball out. Finally he had it in his hand and handed it to Lilibet.

She held it in her hand. "How do I open it?" she asked.

"The ball has two halves," Rolf answered. They are screwed together. Just turn it."

She did as he said. The two halves split apart. There was a piece of paper inside.

"You see?" Rolf said. "I told you."

I. **Complete the sentences with the words from the box below.**

mischief	rough	carved	jovial
impeccably	~~devastated~~	screwed	handled

1. Lilibet was so unhappy that she couldn't do anything but think of her grandfather. She was _devastated_ .

2. But she smiled a little thinking of the _____ they had once gotten into together.

3. Karl Kurz was friendly and cheerful. He had a _____ personality.

4. The road had an uneven surface full of mud and rocks. It was a _____ road.

5. Rolf's truck was made for difficult road conditions. It _____ the rough road very well.

6. Karl Kurz took good care of the cottage. It was tidy and _____ clean.

7. The box was made of wood, and there was a falcon _____ on the lid.

8. The hedgehog had two parts. They were _____ together.

II. Choose two words from the box on the previous page and write a short paragraph using them.

_____
_____
_____
_____

III. Complete the sentences with the expressions from the box below.

split apart	supposed to be
in order to	piggy bank

1. Lilibet had saved some money working part time. She had it in her _____.

2. Lilibet had put the date in the order every American would have. It was as it was _____.

3. There were some moves you had to do _____ get the hedghog out.

4. As Lilibet unsrewed the ball, the two hedgehog halves _____.

IV. Choose two expressions from the box above and write a short paragraph using these expressions.

_____
_____
_____
_____

V. Answer the questions in full sentences.

1. Why was Lilibet devastated?
2. What did her grandfather leave her?
3. Where was her grandfather originally from?
4. Why did he settle in Texas?
5. Where was Lilibet supposed to go and why?
6. Who helped Lilibet?
7. What did Lilibet find in the cottage?
8. What is the Hedgehog in the Cage?
9. What did Lilibet find in the spiky ball?

VI. Oral Summary

Retell the story in a few sentences.

VII. Written Summary

Write a few sentences to summarize the story.

_____
_____
_____
_____
_____
_____
_____
_____

The Texas Rose II

Old Prosek, Czechoslovakia, 1948

The men sat around a wooden table drinking wine and talking. They were talking about politics, and they were very serious. Their worst nightmare had just come true. The communist coup in February 1948 had established a totalitarian regime that would last 41 years. The men were mostly businessmen who had just lost their businesses in the coup. One of the men was Rudolf Zetl, and the party was in his cottage near Prague. Almost all of them agreed that the best solution would be to flee the country and its communist regime as soon as possible.

Rudolf Zetl was there with his 30-year-old son Miles.

"Come Miles," he said suddenly to his son. "We'll go for a little walk." They went outside. They walked in silence for some time and then Rudolf Zetl started to speak.

"I've got something to tell you, son," he said. "I've never talked about it, but now is the time. My father went to America a long time ago. He went there to work to make money for the family. He had a few jobs there. He also worked as a prison guard in Texas. One of the prisoners must have liked him for some reason because when he died, he left my father all his belongings. It wasn't much. He wasn't rich. He had almost nothing. But while he was alive he kept talking about something he had hidden somewhere – something very precious. He said it was the road to eternal happiness. He left a letter with a coded message which contained directions to the place. Unfortunately he didn't tell my father how to crack the code. My father gave the letter to me. He thought that I'd be able to find a way to crack it. I haven't been able to do it. I hope *you* can do it. You must leave the country and go to Texas. I'm too old to go now. Take the letter with the message with you. I put it in the box you carved for my fiftieth birthday. It's hidden in the basement under a tile in the western corner."

Rudolf Zetl didn't have time to tell his son more. Suddenly they heard strange voices near the cottage. "The police," somebody yelled. "Come out one by one with your hands up!"

"Run, Miles, run," Rudolf Zetl whispered to his son. "You must go to Texas as quickly as possible. We'll find a way to get you the coded message later." Miles Zetl ran away. He never saw his father again. But he followed his advice and with help of the right people he made it to Texas just as his father had wanted.

Lilibet unfolded the paper and looked at it. There were no letters, only numbers. She showed it to Rolf. "What do you think about this?" she asked.

"I think it might be a coded message. The paper looks very old so I think the code is simple. Some numbers repeat themselves more than the others. The biggest number is 24. Let's try to change number 1 to A, number 2 to B, number 3 to C and so on."

"I think it's an excellent idea," Lilibet said. "I thought about doing that too."

Rolf got a pen and a piece of paper. They tried changing the numbers to letters as Rolf had said, but the message was incomprehensible.

"It's not the way, Rolf said. "We have to try something else."

Lilibet didn't hear him. She kept looking at the letters.

"It's not possible," she yelled. "It can't be so simple. But it is! Yes!"

"What do you mean," Rolf asked puzzled.

"I used to use this code with my friends when I was a little girl. It's backwards. It's a mirror image."

It didn't take them long, and they were able to read the whole message.

It's the road to eternal happiness. Go to the cold place that belongs to the holder of the heel. The Texas Rose is under the tallest tree – eighteen feet from its center to the north.

"Well," Rolf said. "It's English, but it's still in code – *the cold place, the holder of the heel, the Texas Rose.* Do you know what the Texas Rose is?"

"A Texas rose is a yellow flower that grows only in Texas. But there are many roses like it in Texas. They have no particular value. I don't think the Texas Rose is a flower. We need to go on the Internet. It shouldn't be difficult to break the code."

They got in Rolf's truck and drove back quickly. They went to the library to access the Internet. They both sat at computers next to each other.

"We'll start with *the cold place*," Rolf said. "The first thing that comes to mind is a mountain or a cave. Are there mountains and caves in Texas?"

"Sure, there are many."

Rolf typed *the holder of the heel* in the browser.

"It's from the bible," he said. "It's Jacob. He was born holding his twin brother Esau's heel. There is no Jacob's mountain, but listen to this. There's a place called Jacob's Well in Texas. And it's a cave, a very popular one."

"And I was right," Lilibet said looking at the screen of her computer. "The Texas Rose isn't a flower. It's a diamond of great value. There is a story behind it. An

English nobleman fell in love with a woman from Texas. He gave her the diamond as proof of his love. I don't see any pictures of it, but it must be in the shape of a rose. When the English nobleman died, she gave the diamond to the Dallas Museum of Art. There are no names. The woman wanted to keep it secret. The Texas Rose was stolen from the museum in 1930. It has never been found.

"I love the Internet," Rolf said. "You can find out about so many things in a matter of seconds. Now let's see. We have to go to Jacob's Well in Texas. We'll find the tallest tree near the cave and dig next to it. We'll find the diamond, and we'll be rich." Suddenly he stopped.

"I'm sorry," he said. "I got carried away with excitement. You'll go there, you'll find it, and you'll be rich. It's a gift from your grandfather. It's yours only."

"I'm not so sure that the diamond is only mine," she said with a mischievous smile. "But I've already let you in on the secret. You must go with me. It's our adventure. What do you say?"

Rolf's eyes were shining with excitement. "I say yes."

They spent the next week roaming around Prague. Lilibet loved the old city very much. It was her first time in Europe, so everything was new and exciting. While they were walking through the streets of Prague, they made plans for their adventure in Texas.

A week later they landed at the airport in Dallas. Rolf was so excited. It was his first time in America. Actually it was the first time he had ever been on a plane, so he behaved like a little boy at Christmas. Lilibet's parents welcomed Rolf as cordially as Rolf's grandfather had welcomed their daughter. So Rolf felt at home immediately.

Lilibet took charge of everything. She booked a hotel near the Jacob's Well Natural Area for a week and rented some diving equipment.

"We can do some diving in the cave," she said. "Many people go diving there, so nobody will notice that we're there for another reason."

It was about 200 miles from Dallas to Jacob's Well, so Lilibet drove her convertible there. They got to their hotel about noon. After checking in, they drove to the cave. When they got there, they looked at each other in disappointment. They were some trees nearby, but all of them seemed to be the same height.

"Now what?" Rolf asked.

"We'll look around," Lilibet said. "And we'll see."

They walked around. There were a lot of people. It was a really beautiful natural area. They saw people with diving equipment going into the cave.

"Tomorrow we're going diving," Lilibet said. We'll have some fun."

There was a little shrine near the cave entrance. Two candles were burning there. They saw it, but they didn't pay much attention to it. They had seen similar shrines many times before – especially near roads.

In the evening they went to the restaurant in their hotel for dinner. They met another young couple there and started to talk with them. They talked about Jacob's Well and diving. The other couple came to Jacob's Well almost every year to dive.

"I've been here once before," Lilibet said. "But I haven't been here for five years."

"No?" the young woman asked. "So you might not know about the tragedy that happened here four years ago."

"What tragedy?" Lilibet asked.

"Two people were killed here. Didn't you notice a little shrine near the entrance to the cave?"

"I did," Lilibet said. "What happened to them?"

"There was a strong wind. The wind uprooted a giant tree. The tree fell down. It fell on two people. They were killed instantly. Can you believe it? Somebody should have gone to prison for it. The tree was at least sixty feet higher than the other trees around, and nobody did anything about it. It should have been cut down a long time ago."

Rolf and Lilibet looked at each other. "It's incredible," they said almost at the same time. "Something definitely should have been done about it."

When they were finally alone, Lilibet said, "Tomorrow we'll go diving, and we'll look at the place where that giant tree used to grow."

The next day they went diving, and it was a lot of fun for them. After that they walked around looking for the place. It didn't take them long to find it. The place where the tree had been was now a little shrine with some flowers. They looked around. There was nobody near them. Rolf took out a measuring tape and Lilibet her iphone. She launched the compass app.

"This way," she said.

Rolf quickly measured 18 feet to the north and put three little pebbles at the place. "We have to dig here," he said. "We'll do it tonight."

At midnight they were back at the place. It was dark, and nobody was around. They waited and listened for any suspicious sounds. There was total silence.

"I don't like it at all," Lilibet said. "I'm scared, and I feel like a thief."

"We haven't stolen anything," Rolf said. "At least not yet, and we can't stop now. Let's do it."

She switched on a flashlight, and he started to dig with a shovel. Surprisingly the earth was not hard, and fifteen minutes later the shovel hit something hard.

"I think we've got it," Rolf whispered happily. He sped up the digging, and five minutes later he took a wooden box out of the hole.

"It was easier than I thought," he said and started to clean the box. It was a simple wooden box with no inscription. There was a metal lock on it.

"We haven't got the key," Rolf said. "But it won't be difficult to break the lock."

Suddenly a bright light coming from a powerful flashlight was aimed directly at them. Two men were looking at them. One of them had a gun.

"Put the box down and step back," the man with the gun said.

Rolf hesitated. "Who are you?" he asked. "Are you the police?"

"They're not the police," Lilibet said. "But give them the box, Rolf. They're dangerous. I recognize the gang tattoos."

Rolf put the box down and stepped back, but he watched both men very carefully.

One of the men picked up the box while continuing to point his gun at Rolf. The other man grabbed Lilibet. "You're coming with us," he said and started to drag her to their car.

I. **Complete the sentences with the words from the box below.**

| precious | hesitated | shrine | belongings |
| convertible | ~~flee~~ | cordially | suspicious |

1. The people agreed that the best solution would be to _flee_ their home country and to live elsewhere.

2. The man left Lilibet's great-grandfather everything he had. He left him all his _____.

3. Her grandfather left Lilibet something valuable and important. He left her something _____.

4. Lilibet's parents were very nice people. They greeted Rolf _____.

5. Lilibet had a nice car with a retractable roof. She had a _____.

6. There was a cross, two burning candles and some flowers. It looked like a little _____.

7. Rolf and Lilibet listened to see if they were alone. They listened for any _____ sounds.

8. Rolf didn't know if he should obey the man or not. He _____.

II. Choose two words from the box on the previous page and write a short paragraph using them.

_____
_____
_____
_____

III. Complete the sentences with the expressions from the box below.

carried away	crack the code
communist coup	roaming around

1. The communists in Czechoslovakia took power by force. It was a _____.

2. Lilibet didn't know how to read the encoded message. She didn't know how to _____.

3. Rolf started to talk excitedly without thinking. He got _____.

4. Lilibet and Rolf were walking around Prague with no clear purpose. They were _____.

IV. Choose two expressions from the box above and write a short paragraph using these expressions.

_____
_____
_____
_____

V. Answer the questions in full sentences.

1. Why did the men gather in the cottage?
2. What did Rudolf Zetl tell his son Miles?
3. What did Lilibet find in the hedgehog?
4. Why couldn't they read the letter?
5. How did they crack the code?
6. What did the letter say? Did they understand it?
7. How did they figure out what it meant?
8. What did they find near Jacob's Well?
9. What happened at the end?

VI. Oral Summary

Retell the story in a few sentences.

VII. Written Summary

Write a few sentences to summarize the story.

_____
_____
_____
_____
_____
_____
_____
_____

The Texas Rose III

"You've made a mistake," Rolf said.

"What?" the man with the gun asked and laughed.

"You've made a mistake," Rolf repeated. You shouldn't have touched my girlfriend."

"Go to hell," the man said. They were laughing as they approached their car.

Rolf suddenly picked up the shovel with surprising quickness and threw it at the man with the gun. "After you," he shouted.

The shovel hit the man's back knocking him down. He lay on the ground without moving. The gun lay next to him.

The other man let go of Lilibet and ran to grab the gun. As he bent down, Rolf was there and kicked him in the head. Now both men were on the ground. They didn't move. Lilibet was flabbergasted. Did Rolf just knock down two dangerous gang members? He was tall, but skinny. He didn't have big muscles. There's more to this boy than meets the eye, she thought.

"How in the world did you do that?" she asked.

"I got lucky," Rolf said smiling. "I've never knocked anybody down by throwing a shovel at them. But martial arts have been my hobby since I was four years old. And I couldn't let them take you away from me, could I?"

"Well, thanks," she said still shaking her head. "You haven't killed them, have you?"

Rolf looked at the men. "No, I haven't," he said. "They're tough guys. They're only knocked out. They'll wake up soon."

He got a knife and cut their car tires. Then he picked up the box. He didn't touch the gun. He left it on the ground.

"We have to run. We don't have much time," he said.

They ran to their car, got in and drove away. They checked out of the hotel and soon they were on their way to Dallas. The box was hidden in the trunk.

They got home early in the morning. They were exhausted.

"Are we going to open it?" Rolf asked. "I can hardly wait."

"No," Lilibet said. "Let's sleep on it. Good night, and thanks again."

He came up to her. He stood upright trying to make himself look taller than he really was. "Don't mention it," he said. "It was nothing."

"Sure," she said smiling. She looked at him for a minute. Then she turned around and went to her room.

He stood there for a while looking at the closed door. Then he turned around and went to his room too. Ten minutes later they were both asleep.

Rolf woke up and opened his eyes. It was about noon. It took him a while to realize he was not at home in Prague, but in Dallas. He had dreamt about a yellow rose. In his dream he had fought with two men over a yellow rose. He won the fight and gave the rose to a girl. Was she Lilibet? He couldn't tell. He wasn't sure. The girl accepted the rose and gave him a kiss. But the girl was sad, because he had to leave her for some time. "Don't leave me," she said. And then he woke up.

He went down to the kitchen. Lilibet was there making some food.

"Good morning," she said. I've prepared some food for us. We're going to have a picnic. I know a nice place. There aren't usually many people there. We're going to open our box there. What do you say?"

"I say yes," Rolf answered.

"Take along some tools so you can break the lock," Lilibet said.

They drove for a time in silence. They both had a lot to think about.

"What do you think is in the box?" Rolf asked breaking the silence.

"The Texas Rose, the famous diamond," she said. "At least I hope so. And what do you think?"

"I really don't know," Rolf said. "I just hope there's something that will make you happy." He sounded a little bit sad.

She looked at him, but didn't say anything.

Lilibet stopped and killed the engine. "We're here," she said.

Rolf got out of the car and looked around. There was a beautiful lake surrounded by woods. "Beautiful," he said, "just beautiful. I'm speechless. I didn't know Texas was so amazing."

"I brought you here to show you we have beautiful places here, too," Lilibet said.

Rolf looked at her. "I've never doubted it."

They sat on a blanket and ate some food. Then Lilibet said, "It's time."

Rolf got up and went to the car to get a power drill. The lock broke easily under the drill. He handed the box to Lilibet.

"Here you are," he said.

She closed her eyes and opened the box.

"What is it?" she asked.

"Another box," Rolf said. "A smaller one, but it looks like a jewelry box."

She opened her eyes, took out the jewelry box, closed her eyes again and opened the jewelry box.

"What is it?" she asked.

There was long silence. "Hello, are you there?" she asked still with her eyes closed.

"Yes, I'm here," he said. "It looks like a diamond, a big one. But it's not in the shape of a rose. It's a heart."

"Lilibet opened her eyes. "Wow," she said. "It's beautiful."

They looked at it in silence for a long time.

"Look," Lilibet said. "There's a golden plate with something written on it. She read:

For my Texas Rose
You stole my heart a long time ago, and you still have it. It's forever yours.

"He didn't sign his name," Lilibet said. "Their love must have been a secret. I think they loved each other very much. Now I understand. The Englishman called his love the Texas Rose. Maybe her name was Rose or he meant the flower. We'll never know. They named the diamond after her."

"Well, now it's yours. What are you going to do with it?" Rolf asked.

"It's not mine," she said. "And it never will be. It belongs to somebody else. It's too personal. I don't want it."

"What are you going to do with it?" Rolf asked again.

"I'm going to return the Texas Rose to where it was meant to be – the museum."

"But they're going to ask you questions. How are you …"

"No, they're not. I'm going to mail it."

"But it's not safe," Rolf said. "It's a very expensive jewel, and they might not get it."

"Well, I'm going to take the risk," Lilibet said. "They wouldn't have gotten it anyway if we hadn't found it, would they?"

"No, they wouldn't have, I guess." Rolf said. "I get it."

There a little sadness in Rolf's voice, and Lilibet noticed it.

"I understand," she said. "All that treasure hunting, and in the end you have nothing, but I ..."

"It's not true," Rolf said loudly.

"What's not true?" Lilibet asked.

"That I have nothing," he said. "I found my own Texas Rose during our treasure hunt."

"Really?" she said. "And where's your Texas Rose?"

"She's right here speaking to me."

Lilibet was silent. She didn't say anything. She looked at Rolf. Tears appeared in her eyes and shone in the sun. "I'm so sorry that our adventure is ending," she said sadly.

A week later Lilibet and Rolf were at the Dallas airport. Rolf was going home to Prague. Boarding was in ten minutes.

"Am I imagining it or have you wanted to tell me something for the last two hours?" Lilibet asked.

"No, you're not imagining it," Rolf answered.

"So, what is it? Your flight is in eight minutes. Tell me."

"OK," Rolf said. He finally found the courage. "What do you think about long distance relationships?"

"I don't know," she said smiling. "I haven't tried one yet."

"OK," Rolf said. "Let me start again. Do you want to be my girlfriend? I'd be very happy if the answer is yes."

"But *I am* your girlfriend," Lilibet said. "Have you forgotten what you said to those thugs that attacked us? *You've made a mistake. You shouldn't have touched my girlfriend.* It sounded so good. I thought you really meant it, and I was happy."

"I'll take that as a yes," Rolf said.

They both started to laugh. They laughed and laughed – two young hearts in love. Then they kissed for the first time. They both hoped it wouldn't be for the last time.

Rolf was at the airport in Paris. He was sitting in a café waiting for his flight. He picked up his cup of coffee. He was about to take a sip when suddenly he put the cup down.

"Excuse me," he called to the waitress staring at the TV screen. "Could you turn the sound up for a minute?"

The waitress turned the sound up and disappeared.

"Breaking news," the announcer said. "Something unbelievable happened. A suspicious package was delivered to the Dallas Museum of Art this morning. The bomb squad was called to the museum. There were no bombs or dangerous substances inside. There was a jewel – a diamond in the shape of a heart. The value of the diamond is estimated at $2,000,000. Somebody who obviously didn't want to disclose their identity sent it by mail. The diamond has a name – the Texas Rose. Somebody has returned the diamond stolen from the museum 65 years ago. Isn't that amazing? We can say that the Texas Rose – the diamond heart, the symbol of love and eternal happiness, has finally found its way home."

Rolf was staring at the TV screen with a big smile on his face.

"What are you smiling about?" the waitress asked.

"About the news," Rolf said. It reminded me of something ... and somebody I love. I'm smiling because I'm happy.

Lilibet was at home in the living room watching TV. She had just heard the news about the Texas Rose. She had a big smile on her face. Her father walked into the living room.

"What are you smiling about?" he asked her.

"You would never believe what I did, Daddy," she said. "I'm smiling because I am so happy."

I. **Complete the sentences with the words from the box below.**

bomb squad	staring	speechless	sip
~~flabbergasted~~	thugs	disclose	martial arts

1. Lilibet was shocked. She was _flabbergasted_.

2. Rolf was interested in fighting techniques. He was interested in _____.

3. The countryside was so beautiful that Rolf didn't know what to say. He was _____.

4. The two men were violent criminals. They were _____.

5. Rolf wanted to drink a little bit of his coffee. He wanted to take a _____.

6. Rolf was looking at the TV sceen. He was hypnotized by what he saw. He was _____ at the screen.

7. Some people came to open the suspicious package. They thought there might be a bomb inside. They were from the _____.

8. The person who sent the package didn't want anybody to know who he was. He didn't want to _____ his identity.

II. **Choose two words from the box on the previous page and write a short paragraph using them.**

_____
_____
_____
_____

III. **Complete the sentences with the expressions from the box below.**

don't mention it	let's sleep on it
killed the engine	than meets the eye

1. Lilibet didn't know what to expect from Rolf. There was more to him _____.

2. Lilibet wanted to open the box the following day. She said, "_____."

3. Rolf wanted to tell Lilibet that it was not necessary to thank him. He said, "_____."

4. Lilibet stopped her car. She turned the key and took it out. She _____.

IV. **Choose two expressions from the box above and write a short paragraph using them.**

_____
_____
_____
_____

V. Answer the questions in full sentences.

1. What did Rolf do to save Lilibet?
2. How did she feel about it?
3. Where did Lilibet and Rolf go to open the box?
4. What was inside the wooden box?
5. What was inside the jewelry box?
6. Who did the Texas Rose belong to?
7. Who did the woman get the diamond from?
8. What did Lilibet do with the diamond?
9. How did Lilibet and Rolf feel in the end?

VI. Oral Summary

Retell the story in a few sentences.

VII. Written Summary

Write a few sentences to summarize the story.

_____
_____
_____
_____
_____
_____
_____

FREE AUDIO

You can download a free audio version of the book at

www.easy-reading-esl.com/freedownload9798637.html

NOTES

Printed in Great Britain
by Amazon